COLOPHON

We made this Flow Book for Paper Lovers

Creative Director Irene Smit
Art Director Karin Sonneveld
Creative Managing Editor Caroline Buijs
Design & Layout Joyce Zethof♥
General Managing Editor Maaike Beekers
Coordinating Editor Floor Zijp
Translation Elise Reynolds♥
Copy Editor Julia Gorodecky♥
Image & Rights Coordinator Marjolijn Polman
Online Coordinator Ruby Wijdenbosch
Editorial Assistance Benthe Aardenburg, Julia Houtermans, Noa Kieviet (trainees), Nadie van Moorselaar♥
♥ **freelance**

Postal address Flow, Spaklerweg 53, 1114 AE Amsterdam, the Netherlands
E-mail redactie.flowmagazine@roularta.nl

CONTRIBUTORS♥
Cynthia Borst, Michael Doyle, Floortje Louise, Holly Jolley Massaro, Léa Le Pivert, Aino Salo, Deborah van der Schaaf, Karen Schipper, Ashley Seil Smith, Ruby Taylor

CEO Marjolein Denekamp
Director Magazines Léon Bouwman

SALES
Roularta Media Nederland
+31 (0)20 2105459
advertising@roularta.nl

Creative founders Astrid van der Hulst and Irene Smit

FLOW BOOK FOR PAPER LOVERS IS A SPECIAL EDITION OF FLOW MAGAZINE FROM THE NETHERLANDS
Flowmagazine.nl & Flowmagazine.com

FLOW BOOK FOR PAPER LOVERS is a special edition of Flow Magazine from the Netherlands. Flow Specials are published by Roularta Media Nederland, a member of the Dutch Publishers Association (Consumer Magazines Group), Spaklerweg 53, 1114 AE Amsterdam, the Netherlands.

DISTRIBUTION
For more information about selling Flow products, please contact: ingrid.pronk@roularta.nl

LICENSING & SYNDICATION
The Flow brand is available for International Licensing and Syndication. For more information, please contact: ingrid.pronk@roularta.nl

NIEUWE ABONNEMENTEN
Bel 088-5500121, ma t/m vrij 9.00-21.00 uur. Of kijk op Flowmagazine.nl/abonnementen.

KLANTENSERVICE
Voor vragen over opzeggen, bezorgen, betaling, wijzigingen, welkomstgeschenken en artikelen. Telefoon: 088-5500121 (Nederland), +32-24542910 (België) (ma t/m vrij 9.00-21.00 uur). E-mail: customerservice.info@dpgmedia.nl. Adreswijzigingen dienen drie weken voor de verhuizing bij ons bekend te zijn. Beëindigen van het abonnement kan tegen het einde van de eerste abonnementstermijn, door uiterlijk een maand voor verschijnen van het eerste nummer van de nieuwe abonnementstermijn bij Roularta Media Nederland op te zeggen. Na de eerste abonnementstermijn kan het abonnement met inachtneming van een opzegtermijn van een maand worden beëindigd. Verschenen nummers kunnen tot twee edities terug worden nabesteld. Beëindiging van de e-mail nieuwsbrief kan via de afmeldlink onder in de nieuwsbrief, of door een verzoek te sturen aan privacy@roularta.nl.

DISTRIBUTIE LOSSE VERKOOP
Aldipress (Nederland), AMP (België) B.V.

LEESPORTEFEUILLE
Zonder schriftelijke toestemming van de uitgever is opname van deze uitgave in een leesportefeuille niet toegestaan.

ABONNEMENTSPRIJZEN
Voor actuele abonnementstarieven zie Flowmagazine.nl/abonnementen.

LEVERINGSVOORWAARDEN
Levering van tijdschriften en levering en verkoop van premies en handelsartikelen geschiedt volgens de Leveringsvoorwaarden Roularta Media Nederland. Kijk voor deze voorwaarden op Roularta.nl/voorwaarden. Voor alle premies, aanbiedingen en acties in Nederland en België geldt: zolang de voorraad strekt. Helaas is het bestellen van handelsartikelen niet mogelijk vanuit landen buiten Nederland en België.

PRIVACY
Roularta Media Nederland, de uitgever van Flow, legt van haar abonnees en klanten in het kader van haar dienstverlening gegevens vast. Deze persoonsgegevens worden verwerkt in overeenstemming met de toepasselijke wet- en regelgeving, waaronder de Algemene Verordening Gegevensbescherming (AVG). Kijk voor het privacybeleid van Roularta Media Nederland op Roularta.nl/privacyvoorwaarden. Via het e-mailadres privacy@roularta.nl kun je contact opnemen als je vragen hebt over dit privacybeleid.

Roularta Media Nederland

HOI 2025 KEURMERK

mma magazine media associatie

LOST IN ILLUSTRATIONS

The best thing about creating something yourself? For me, it's the fact that I can lose myself in it completely, forgetting all about time—as if the world around me has stopped for a moment. Paper is my favorite material: it's such a versatile basis for creativity. Each of the illustrators who contributed to this issue of the Flow Book for Paper Lovers started with a blank page of paper that patiently waited to be transformed into a small work of art. And now that you're holding this book in your hands, you can see and feel how their creativity and efforts have created something that you can enjoy and cherish. I love the thought that everybody will do something different with this book and all its detachable pages and paper goodies. One thing's for sure: letters will be written, cards will be posted, gifts will be wrapped and stickers will be stuck. But there's more: letter fonts, flowers, cats and the many other artworks can be cut out to make collages. All these pages of illustrations can be used to fold into little books and envelopes, or to paint and draw on, or to paste all over your journal. And every time you lose yourself in this book, you'll be spending time away from screens and social media for a while. The good news is that research shows people who engage in creative activities have higher ratings for happiness and on having a sense of purpose in life. All in all, creating something yourself provides you with fresh energy and relaxation at the same time. This book is your doorway to that. So, enjoy!

Het fijnst aan zelf iets maken? Dat ik er helemaal in opga en de tijd vergeet – alsof de wereld om me heen even niet meer bestaat. Papier is mijn favoriete materiaal: het is zo'n veelzijdig startpunt voor creativiteit. Bij de illustratoren in deze editie van het Book for Paper Lovers begon het met een lege pagina die geduldig wachtte om omgetoverd te worden tot een klein kunstwerk. En nu jij dit boek in handen hebt, kun je zien en ervaren hoe hun creativiteit en inspanning heeft geleid tot iets wat je kunt vasthouden en koesteren. Ik vind het zo'n tof idee dat iedereen iets anders gaat doen met dit boek vol uitscheurbare pagina's en paper goodies. Er worden zeker weten brieven geschreven, kaartjes verstuurd, cadeaus ingepakt en stickers geplakt. Maar ook: letters, bloemen, katten en andere illustraties uitgeknipt om collages mee te maken. Al die vellen met illustraties kun je verwerken tot boekjes en enveloppen, je kunt erop schilderen en tekenen of je journal mee volplakken. En steeds wanneer je in dit boek duikt, ben je even weg van een scherm en van social media. Goed nieuws: onderzoek wijst uit dat mensen die creatief bezig zijn, hoger scoren op geluk en het gevoel een zinvol leven te leiden. Kortom: zelf iets maken geeft energie en ontspant tegelijk. Dit boek helpt je daarbij.

Veel plezier!

Caroline

Creative managing editor

ABOUT FLOW

Flow celebrates unhurried days, creativity and living consciously.
Flow Magazine is available in English, Dutch, German and French. What's more, we also create Books for Paper Lovers!

Flowmagazine.com
@flow_magazine

Flowmagazine.nl
@flow_magazine

Flow-magazin.de
@flow_magazin

Flowmagazine.fr
@flowmagazine_fr

Twice a year, we create a book filled with paper goodies.
You'll find our latest issues on flowmagazine.com

MEET THE DESIGNERS

CYNTHIA BORST

Purmerend, the Netherlands

I am: A theatre designer and illustrator.
My contribution to this book: Nature drawings using old paper and a (digital) pencil.
My working process: Most of the time, I start by thinking about what I want to convey. Based on that, I make a sketch that I'm often dissatisfied with. I'll put it to the side and look at it again a day later. Usually, it turns out to be spot-on and I hardly have to do anything more to it.
My inspiration: A stain, fold or tear that's in the paper. Like in the illustration with the heron: the lines on the page were already ripples in the water; I only needed to add a few lines to bring it to life.
What paper means to me: I love old paper items as they already have such life in them. @cynthiaborst

HOLLY JOLLEY MASSARO

London, UK

I am: An artist and designer.
My contribution to this book: Animal scenes and floral patterns.
My working process: I create ink line drawings and gouache paintings.
My inspiration: Nature, specks of domestic bliss, literature and fashion.
What paper means to me: It's a medium for preserving and translating experiences. Concrete evidence that the world, ideas, beauty and stories do, in fact, exist. @ceres.archives

ASHLEY SEIL SMITH

New York, US

I am: An illustrator and painter.
My contribution to this book: A collection of abstract patterns and spot illustrations.
My working process: I go back and forth between analog and digital methods, and love playing with abstraction and transparency. I'm always surrounded by my dogs and cats when I work.
My inspiration: Psychology, women and the natural world.
What paper means to me: Paper means endless possibility. Since its invention, it has held countless ideas and creations through word and image. It's one of the best tools for creativity. @seilsmith

RUBY TAYLOR
Bristol, UK

I am: An illustrator and designer.
My contribution to this book: A bright and cheerful birthday calendar.
My working process: I usually start by building ideas or layouts in a sketchbook, and then I work digitally in Photoshop.
My inspiration: I love old, printed ephemera, vintage advertising, folk art and bright color palettes.
What paper means to me: Paper is always inspiring, whether it's a blank page waiting to be filled or something colorful waiting to be made into something new. @rubyst

FLOORTJE LOUISE
Haarlem, the Netherlands

I am: A photographer with a huge passion for nature.
My contribution to this book: Photos that draw upon my fascination for light and shadow.
My working process: I work intuitively and rarely ever plan anything in advance. When I do, the result is never as expected.
My inspiration: The subtle beauty of nature. And the moments when a flower or plant seems to be more than just its shape.
What paper means to me: Paper is the ultimate canvas, a blank surface from which anything can emerge. @floortje.louise; @isu.archives

KAREN SCHIPPER
Greenville, US

I am: An illustrator and paper goods designer who creates joyful illustrations.
My contribution to this book: Four patterns in blue and a touch of ochre.
My working process: I paint in Photoshop.
My inspiration: Nature, colors and vintage picture books.
What paper means to me: Although most of my work is created digitally, almost all of it is created for paper products. I think through paper—nothing can replace putting your thoughts down on paper with ink or writing a handwritten note. @karen.schipper

MICHAEL DOYLE
Seattle, US

I am: A painter (who loves to read).
My contribution to this book: Bright and curious illustrations, such as a watchful squirrel, a marble apple and a cat with a secret.
My working process: It's kind of all over the place and erratic. But, I do go to my studio every day and I like it to be tidy. Brian Eno talks about catching creative thoughts by cleaning your studio and I think he's onto something.
My inspiration: It can be all sorts of things, but mostly from the books I read. I love biographies on artists, Agatha Christie mysteries and cookbooks.
What paper means to me: I love paper. I love ephemera. The only things I collect are paper. I have vintage suitcases filled with zines, art show flyers, postcards, cut-out scraps. I could never throw any of them away. All those memories… they tell the story of my life. @michaeldoylestudio

LÉA LE PIVERT

Brest, France

I am: A freelance illustrator who finds joy in creating comforting and peaceful scenes.
My contribution to this book: Patterns in the theme of a cozy cat café.
My working process: I typically start with a rough sketch and then refine the shapes and colors on my iPad. My favorite part is adding hand-painted details and textures to bring the illustrations to life. This adds depth and a touch of imperfection that's hard to achieve digitally.
My inspiration: I love cafés that feel like a second home—a place to read a good book on a comfy couch, spend the entire day working and eat delicious pastries. And it's even better if there are cats around…
What paper means to me: Paper always marks the beginning of something—it's a blank canvas where anything can happen, whether it's a piece of art, a love letter, or a grocery shopping list. @lealepivert

AINO SALO

Helsinki, Finland

I am: An illustrator and pattern designer who loves creating bold, nature-inspired designs.
My contribution to this book: Four floral patterns and five stand-alone floral illustrations.
My working process: I start with studying and photographing nature, then make loose sketches and refine them digitally. In the final stage, I love experimenting with colors and details to bring my designs to life.
My inspiration: Nature, bold color palettes, and the small, beautiful details I find in everyday life.
What paper means to me: For me, paper transforms designs into keepsakes, making creativity something you can hold and treasure. @byainosalo

DEBORAH VAN DER SCHAAF

Lekkerkerk, the Netherlands

I am: An illustrator.
My contribution to this book: A lift-the-flap Flow Arts & Crafts Store and three large envelopes.
My working process: I start by making rough sketches and then work on them further in the material that best suits the assignment. Finally, I do the fine-tuning and post-processing digitally.
My inspiration: The exhibitions of, and interviews with, other creatives.
What paper means to me: I recently joined a foundation that supports and showcases (hand) printing (letterpress), because paper and the craft of printing are close to my heart. @deborahvanderschaaf

N° 84

N° 84

N° 84

Nº 84

STAY STRONG

MISS YOU

ENJOY YOUR TRAVELS

flow

ILLUSTRATION **CYNTHIA BORST**

flow

ILLUSTRATION **CYNTHIA BORST**

flow

ILLUSTRATION **CYNTHIA BORST**

flow

ILLUSTRATION **CYNTHIA BORST**

ILLUSTRATION **HOLLY JOLLEY**

ILLUSTRATION **HOLLY JOLLEY**

ILLUSTRATION **HOLLY JOLLEY**

ENJOY!

FOR YOU

WITH LOVE

YOU'RE A RAY OF LIGHT

JANUARY

1	2	3	4	5	6
7	8	9	10	11	12
13	14	15	16	17	18
19	20	21	22	23	24
25	26	27	28	29	30
31					

1	2	3	4	5	6
7	8	9	10	11	12

FEBRUARY

13	14	15	16	17	18
19	20	21	22	23	24
25	26	27	28	29	

MARCH

1	2	3	4	5	6
7	8	9	10	11	12
13	14	15	16	17	18
19	20	21	22	23	24
25	26	27	28	29	30
31					

APRIL
1
2
3
4
5
6
7
8
9
10
11
12
13
14
15
16
17
18
19
20
21
22
23
24
25
26
27
28
29
30

May

1	2	3	4	5	6
7	8	9	10	11	12
13	14	15	16	17	18
19	20	21	22	23	24
25	26	27	28	29	30
31					

JUNE

1	2	3	4	5	6
7	8	9	10	11	12
13	14	15	16	17	18
19	20	21	22	23	24
25	26	27	28	29	30

1	2	3	4	5	6
7	8	9	10	11	12

JULY

13	14	15	16	17	18
19	20	21	22	23	24
25	26	27	28	29	30
31					

AUGUST

1	2	3	4
5	6	7	8
9	10	11	12
13	14	15	16
17	18	19	20
21	22	23	24
25	26	27	28
29	30	31	

SEPTEMBER

1	2	3	4	5	6
7	8	9	10	11	12
13	14	15	16	17	18
19	20	21	22	23	24
25	26	27	28	29	30

OCTOBER

1	2	3	4	5
6	7	8	9	10
11	12	13	14	15
16	17	18	19	20
21	22	23	24	25
26	27	28	29	30
				31

NOVE MBER

1	2	3	4	5	6
7	8	9	10	11	12
13	14	15	16	17	18
19	20	21	22	23	24
25	26	27	28	29	30

DECEMBER

1	2	3	4	5	6
7	8	9	10	11	12

13	14	15	16	17	18
19	20	21	22	23	24
25	26	27	28	29	30
31					

JANUARY

FEBRUARY

MARCH

APRIL

MAY

JUNE

JULY

AUGUST

SEPTEMBER

OCTOBER

NOVE
MBER

DECEMBER

FROM ME
TO YOU

POST

hello sunshine

POST

POST

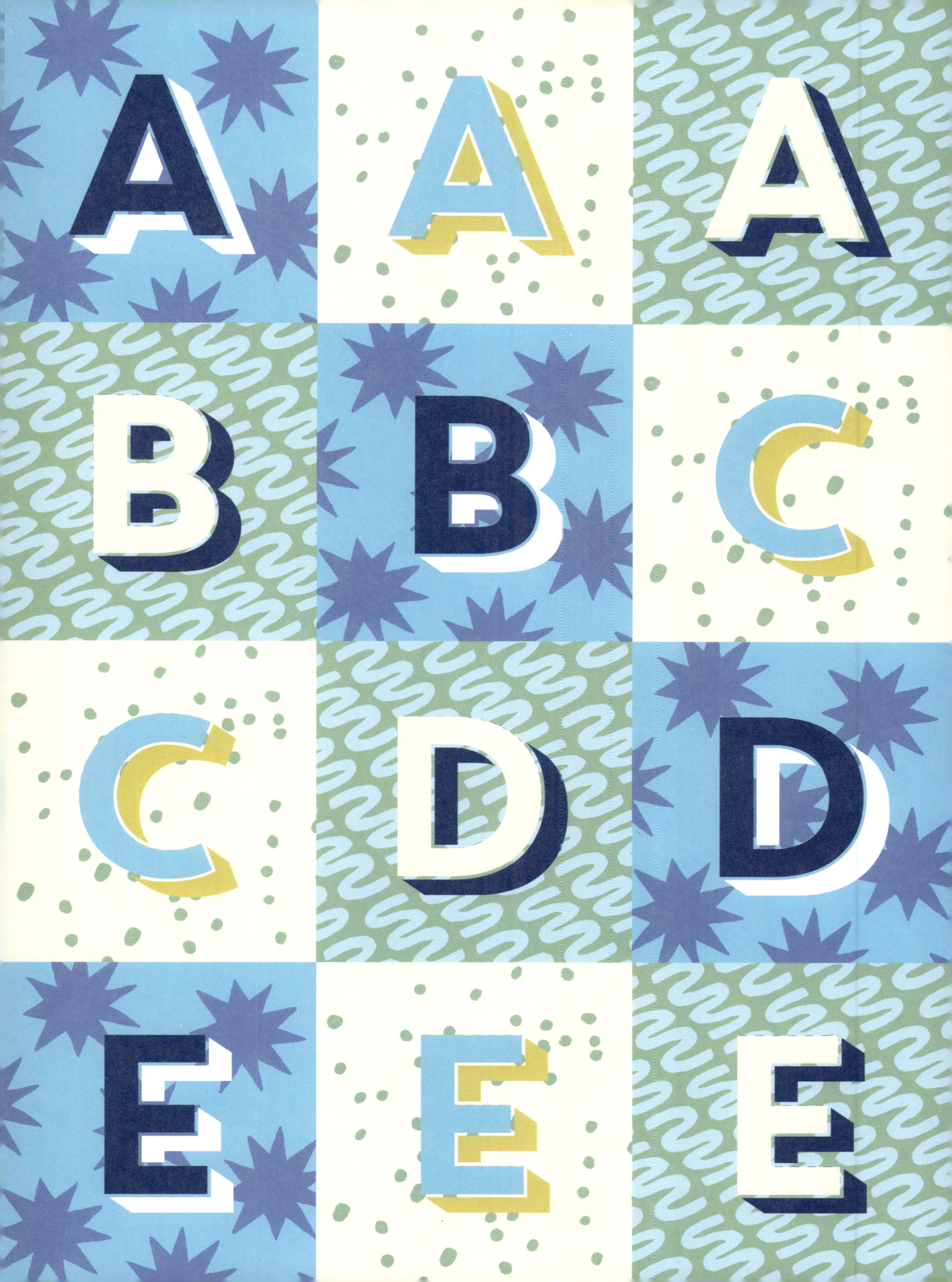
A A A
B B C
C D D
E E E

F F G
G H H
I I J
J K K

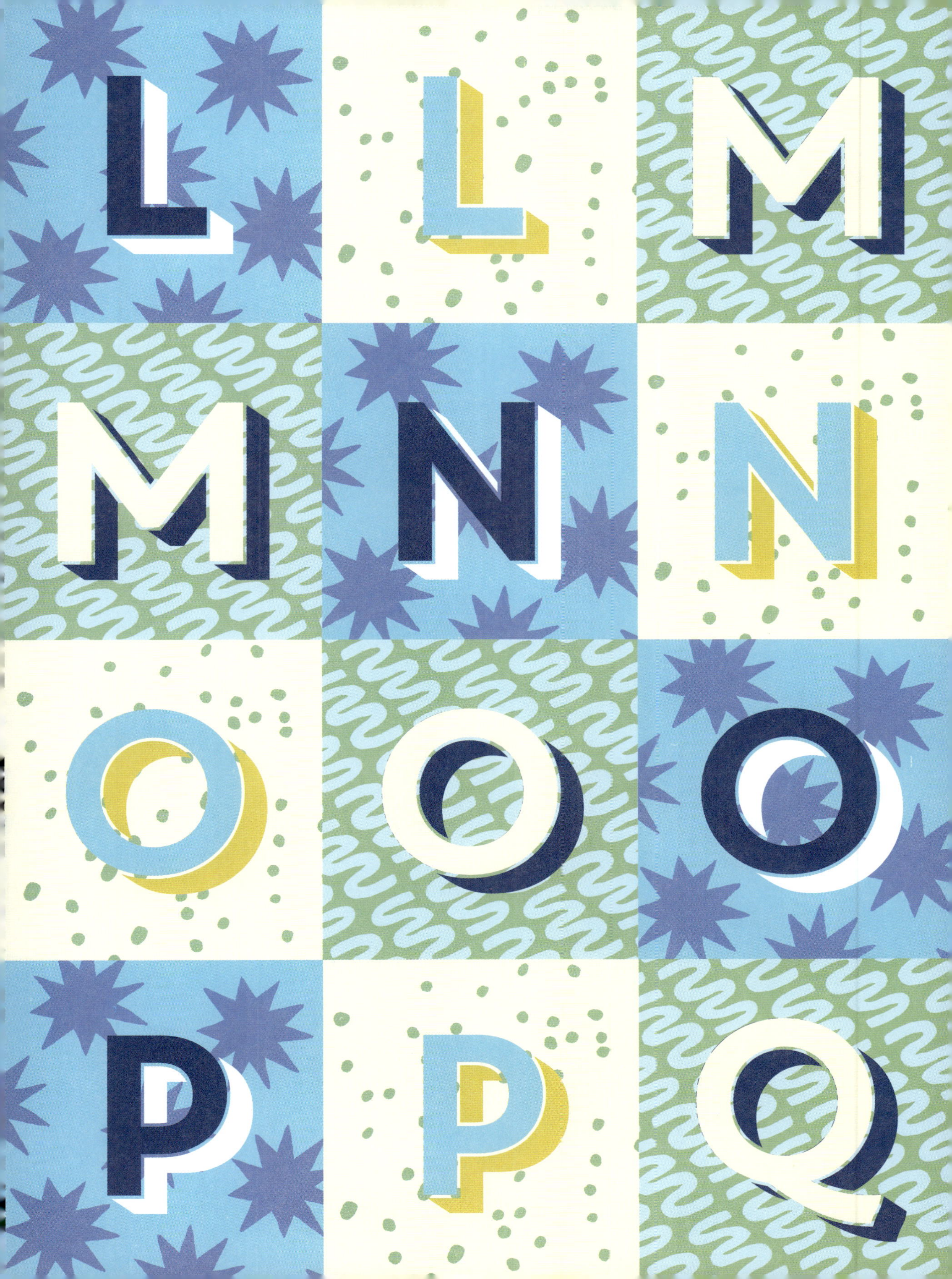
L L M
M N N
O O O
P P Q

R R S
S T U
V W X
Y Z Z

A A B B C C
D D E E E F
F G G H H H
I I J K L L
L M N N N O
O O P P Q R
R R S S T T
U V W X Y Z

BB
IZZY
THEO

Doyle

IZZY
THEO

IZZY
THEO

IZZY
THEO

BB
IZZY
THEO

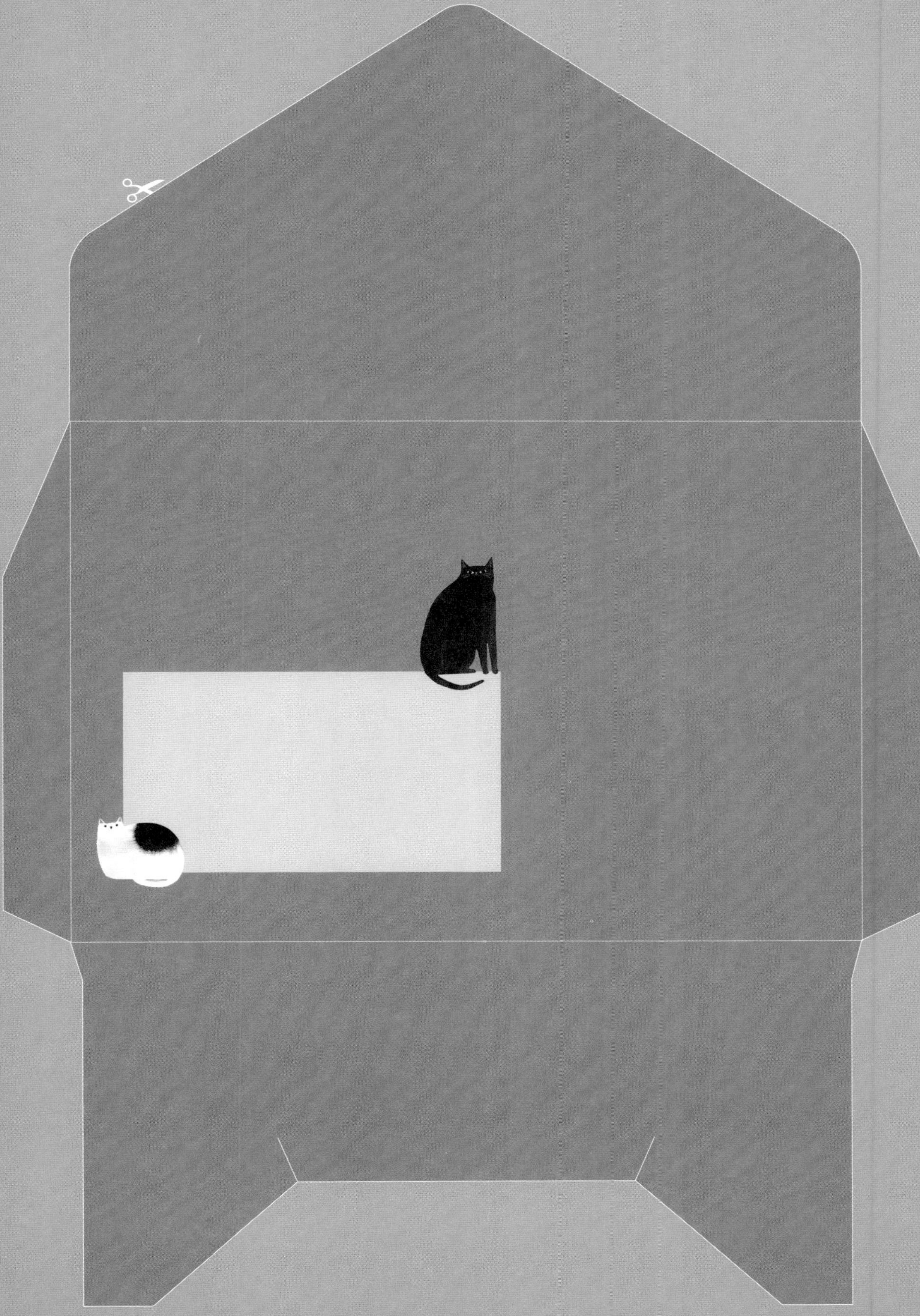

BLOOM
BE OFFBEAT
WE WEIRD
BLOSSOM
GROW GROW GROW GROW GROW GROW
BE YOU
BLOSSOM
BE YOU
FLOURISH
GROW GROW GROW GROW GROW GROW
EMBRACE THE CHAOS
QUIRKY CLUB
QUIRKY CLUB
BE OFF-BEAT
BE WEIRD
BE WEIRD
BLOOM

HERE'S A SPRINKLE OF LUCK

THINKING OF YOU

Hope it all goes well

flow

ILLUSTRATION **AINO SALO**

flow

ILLUSTRATION **AINO SALO**

flow

ILLUSTRATION **AINO SALO**

flow

ILLUSTRATION **AINO SALO**